Lidice

Remembered Around the World

by
Toni Brendel

Front cover:
Dedication pageant at Lidice Monument in Phillips, Wisconsin, U.S.A. The monument was dedicated to liberty, humanity, and justice to all people of the world on August 27, 1944.

Seated in left front row: Sedonia Mencl, Patsy Houdek
Seated far right: George Koci, Sokol member
Second row, behind two girls: Bess Staroba
Behind spinning wheel: Angela Kurka, Victoria Hajny
Third row, left to right: Dorothy Chrusciel, Rose Vojtech, Bessie Soul, Lillian Rehak, and Emily Koci
Placing evergreen spray on monument: Emily Kubat
Back row: Patsy Sova, Lillian Minar, Emily Vojtech, and Betty Ondrejka

Editor: David Wright
Copy Editors: Joan Liffring-Zug Bourret, Deb Schense, and Melinda Bradnan

Graphic Design: M. A. Cook

Back cover photo credits:
Tami Satre photographed the back cover rose in the Garden of Friendship and Peace, Lidice, Czech Republic.
Michael Hladilek photographed the monument with the three flags shown on the back cover.

Title page:
The rose symbolizes new life in the village of Lidice.

Printed in the U. S. A.
Copyright © 2013, 2015 by Toni Brendel

Library of Congress: 2013936930
Second edition: ISBN: 978-1511940955

CONTENTS

Acknowledgments 1

Preface 3

Introduction 4

Prelude to Disaster 8

Villains and Heroes 9

Assassination and its Aftermath 13

The Reprisal 15

A Shocked World 17

Kindred Spirits in the United States 18
    Pittsburgh, Pennsylvania 18
    Phillips, Wisconsin 18
    Chicago, Illinois 37
    Lidice (now Crest Hill), Illinois 38
    Tabor, South Dakota 44

Other Nations Remember Lidice 45
    Stoke-on-Trent, Great Britain 45
    Lidice, Brazil 46
    Others in the World Remember 49

Lidice Today and Tomorrow 51

Epilogue 58

Notes 64

About the Author 65

DEDICATION

This book is dedicated to the people of Lidice and Ležáky and to all those around the world who remember them.

ACKNOWLEDGMENTS

The author gratefully acknowledges the assistance and support of Ivona Kasalicka, curator of the International Children's Exhibition of Fine Art, Lidice; and many thanks to all staff members at the museum and gallery there who made my recent visit to Lidice very special. Many thanks as well to Mayor Veronika Kellerova, Vice Mayor Tomas Skala, and Lidice "children," Marie Supikova and Vaclav Zelenka. Their warmth and generosity will always be remembered.

I am indebted to those who make websites available to the public. The websites of the Lidice Memorial, Czech Republic, the United States Central Intelligence Agency, and the Holocaust Museum were helpful in verifying historical data about the Lidice tragedy. I am also indebted to Eduard Stehlik for his excellent books about Lidice. Due to his access to Czechoslovak military archives, his publications are among the most reliable resources available regarding Lidice and what happened there in the summer of 1942.

I also wish to thank His Excellency, Petr Gandalovic, Czech Ambassador to the United States and his assistant, Ms. Pavlina Ciorobea; the Czech Ministry of Culture and its staffers Dr. Barbara Karpetova, Jiri Ellinger, and Dr. Robert Rehak for their interest, support, and assistance. Some of their helpful efforts date back several years.

In America, thanks are due to *The Bee*, in Phillips, Wisconsin, for the use of information and photographs that appeared in their past issues. Many thanks as well to Nick Churnovic, former mayor of Crest Hill, Illinois; present mayor, Raymond R. Soliman; John Fiala, Lincoln, Nebraska; Tami Satre, Eau Claire, Wisconsin; Michael Hladilek and Bill Ball, Phillips, Wisconsin; Peter Kocemba, University of Zilina, Slovakia, and Michaela Bujnakova, Prague, Czech Republic, for permission to use their photographs.

I am also indebted to Tereze Costa Pinta for information regarding the Lidice Monument in Lidice, Brazil; and to Tanja Bella Sturman, Arlington, Virginia, for sharing information and photographs concerning the Foreign Origin Groups and the "Spirit of Lidice" ambulance plane.

Thanks to Laddie and Carole Zellinger, Chuck and Emily Palka, and Marion Vokurka Young for identifying people on the cover photograph.

Special thanks also to my friends in the Phillips Czechoslovakian Community Festival Committee, who continue to inspire me.

Among family members, I warmly thank my translator, cousin Ivana Broskova; and cousins Ivan, Jr., Matej, and Ivan Brosko, Sr.; Maria and Amalia Broskova; and all my Czech and Slovak relatives for sharing with me the home of my grandparents' birth. Thanks also to my American cousins, Lois Potratz and Mike DeFabio, for understanding my need to walk this walk, and for sometimes walking it with me. Most of all, I thank my children, their spouses, and grandchildren for their love, patience, and encouragement. I am blessed!

—Toni Brendel

PREFACE

The Lidice tragedy must never be forgotten. This book stands as an emphatic call in eternal memory to witness for the people who perished during this ruthless and barbaric moment in history. What happened in Lidice during June 1942 is recorded forever as one of the single worst atrocities of World War II—indeed, the events at Lidice, in the extremity of their savagery, today represent the inhumane and evil acts that occur in every war.

Think of it: the Second World War began at a time when many Czech and Slovak Americans had close personal ties to their homelands. For some, little time had passed since they had emigrated. Loved ones were left behind, but families remained in contact through the written word. The locations of villages and cities in Czech and Slovak lands remained familiar to these new Americans; they could still visualize the homes, churches, schools, and shops that had been left behind. The war had a devastating psychological effect, not only on those suffering in war zones, but also for those in America who anxiously awaited news about the well-being and safety of their families and friends.

This book also describes the lives and actions of those people around the world, even on distant shores, who felt so closely bound to their countrymen that they erected lasting monuments in memory of what happened at Lidice. It is nothing short of phenomenal to realize that today, over seventy years after the catastrophe, there are those who continue to conduct memorial services each year—to honor and remember the village and its martyred men, women, and children.

INTRODUCTION

After World War II ended, my Czech grandparents visited their homeland and brought back soil from old Lidice, the small Bohemian village that was totally destroyed by Nazi SS troops in June 1942. The village men were shot, the women taken to concentration camps, and even the youngest of the children were placed in harm's way. These brutal acts were levied in retaliation for the assassination of one of the most important of Hitler's generals and were meant to halt further resistance to the Nazi regime.

My own association with Lidice began when I was ten years old. Recollection allows that my grandfather came for me one Sunday afternoon, and we rode in his car to our town's Sokol Hall. Here a crowd of people, dressed in black, had congregated. For some reason, my mother had directed me to wear my very best Sunday dress. That particular Sunday afternoon had been chosen for the annual memorial service at the Lidice Monument. The monument had been built near our Sokol Hall four years earlier, to commemorate the village and its people.

Shortly before the ceremony, grandpa came to me with a spoon and a small saucer holding soil. I had not a hint of what was expected of me. He told me to accompany him to the monument, to sprinkle the dirt. Not knowing more than that, I became afraid and refused to do what he asked. He did not coax me, but went away quietly. In retrospect, I knew that he was somehow sad. In later years, an aunt told me that my grandfather had placed my hand in his, and together we had spooned the soil into a small chest. But I have no recollection of that. I know that my dear auntie had a penchant for telling tales. I also have a clear memory of playing on the cement steps and swinging from the iron handrails that led into Sokol Hall. I also recall a grave solemnity that hung in the air that day, with women crying under their black hats.

I have always regretted that I refused my grandfather's request and imagine that he must have been very disappointed. But it was not like him to let on. Long after he died, prompted by a desire to make it up to him in some way, I became interested in the history of the village and its people. I began researching and recording information relating to the tragedy. This created an impetus to learn more about what happened and, eventually, to visit Lidice. In this quest, my Czech roots and the knowledge that my hometown possessed one of only two Lidice monuments in North America guided me along a long path, opening up a new world to me.

My first visit to Lidice did not come about until 1987 when the Communists ruled Czechoslovakia. A friend and I toured Lidice with the distinct feeling of being under watchful eyes. We agreed that a certain tension hung in the air of the Lidice Museum itself. In the basement of the building, a movie was shown which glorified the Russian army for returning the women of Lidice to their village, a village that had ceased to exist. The film gave significant praise to the Communists for rebuilding the village and for awarding a new house to each of those who had survived the massacre.

I later discovered that many of the survivors of the tragedy did not wish to return to the place where their families had been murdered, their houses had been burned and demolished, and their personal belongings had been stolen. Many former residents were forced to come back; the Communists used their return (and the rebuilding of the village) to their own advantage. Although a great deal of the money used in rebuilding the village had come from miners in Stoke-on-Trent in England, and from other sources, the Communists took the credit. Many Czech citizens disdained the rebuilding of Lidice, being well aware of how the Communists used the project for their own glorification.

During my second visit to Lidice in 1988, I saw little change in the Lidice Museum and the surrounding area. This time I carried a message from my friend, Joseph Ondracek, to a woman he knew who worked at the museum.

Soon after the war, under orders of the Czechoslovak government, Joseph Ondracek led a team to investigate the fate of the children of Lidice. He was to locate survivors and bring them home to Lidice. Seventeen of the 105 children were found and returned—some of them by Joseph himself. Unable to live with Communist ideology, Joseph later defected. He came to America and settled in Milwaukee, Wisconsin. After meeting through a mutual friend, Joseph, his wife, and I became close friends.

Somehow, Joseph had learned that his friend Vera Urbanova worked at the Lidice Museum and asked me to deliver a message to her. When we entered the museum, we were greeted by a woman seated behind a desk. When I questioned, "Vera Urbanova?" she was startled and surprised, but her head nodded up and down. With the aid of my Czech cousin, I delivered my message from Joseph. This produced an immediate response as her face brightened. I quickly pressed a brochure into her hand, a printed pamphlet called "Lidice Lives in Phillips, Wisconsin." A woman standing close by with disapproving eyes, and an air of suspicion, began to move toward us. Sensing that it was impossible to converse freely, we moved away and began to look at the museum's displays. Later, we asked permission to take photographs inside the museum and were given permission. I was able to take a few Polaroids for Mr. Ondracek, and Mrs. Urbanova seemed pleased when we gave her one of the photographs. Still, I had no idea if the photo and brochure we gave her would be confiscated.

My third visit to Lidice took place in 1990, soon after the Berlin Wall crumbled and the non-violent Velvet Revolution played out. I could see changes beginning—not only in Lidice, but all along the countryside in Czechoslovakia. The new government was struggling to rebuild the nation, and citizens were beginning to exhibit a new-found pride in the ownership of houses and property. Entrepreneurs from around the world began flooding into Czechoslovakia. One of the first orders of business at the memorial site in Lidice was the elimination of the Communist signage and propaganda. The changes were immediately noticeable.

My fourth, and most recent, visit to Lidice came in August 2011, when a pre-arranged appointment took place with Lidice's mayor, Veronika Kellerova; vice-mayor, Tomas Skala; museum supervisor, Anco Marinov; and the then-curator of the Lidice Art Gallery, Ivona Kasalicka. After a sad, thought-provoking tour of the museum and grounds, accompanied by several of our hosts, my three cousins and I were treated to a wonderful Czech meal, cooked in the kitchen of the Art Gallery restaurant. Two of the "Lidice children," Vaclav Zelenka and Marie Supikova, joined us for lunch. Afterward, I was able to interview them, with Ivona Kasalicka acting as interpreter.

Following our interview, I was introduced to a young woman who worked in the art gallery. She was the daughter of Vera Urbanova and she told me that her mother treasured the photo that I had given her all those years ago. So do I–and I share a copy of that historic photo at right.

This last visit was, for me, the most memorable. I made many new friendships, and I learned a great deal more about Lidice through these personal connections. As a result of that 2011 visit, I am now able to add to my original writings about Lidice. Thanks to Mr. Zelenka, Mrs. Supikova, and Mrs. Kasalicka, I now know much more about this important history. I am amazed by the people in Lidice who have so conscientiously and lovingly preserved the integrity of the Lidice Memorial. These wonderful people graciously share their knowledge and insights with all those who visit those hallowed grounds. My life has been enriched by them.

Vera Urbanova (left) with Toni Brendel at the Lidice Museum

PRELUDE TO DISASTER

On October 5, 1938, Dr. Edvard Benes, aware that war was imminent, resigned as the president of Czechoslovakia. For reasons of personal safety and at the urging of friends and family, Benes and his wife flew to London following his resignation. When invited to join the faculty at the University of Chicago as a visiting professor, he accepted the invitation, and he and Mrs. Benes traveled to the United States. He toured America, making speeches promoting democracy. Dr. Benes subsequently became acquainted with President Franklin Roosevelt.

Hitler's army was marching across Europe and soon invaded the capital city of Prague. Dr. Benes wanted, more than anything, to save the Republic; he believed that he could best serve his country by returning to Europe. After receiving news of Czechoslovakia's occupation by the Nazis, he and Mrs. Benes flew back to London, where he began to organize a government-in-exile. By 1941, the Czechoslovak Provisional Government was recognized in Great Britain, with Dr. Benes as its president. This recognition was also granted by the other Allied powers soon after that.

President Benes and Czechoslovak military leaders maintained constant contact with resistance fighters in their homeland via radio transmitters hidden mainly in sparsely-populated villages and hamlets. The Czechoslovak army-in-exile trained soldiers at a home base in London, and parachutists were airlifted to Nazi-occupied territories. These soldiers were valuable to the underground movement in Czechoslovakia and to the Allied forces since they knew the languages and were familiar with the terrain of the country.

Throughout the European theatre of war, atrocities abounded as Nazi ideology ran rampant. The resistance movement became less and less effective; innocent victims were tortured and killed at the least suspicion that they did not support the Third Reich. Hitler's fanatical forces seemed unstoppable and, as time wore on, the resistance movement was losing heart. Special attention was drawn to underground resistance, and Hitler put a plan in place to destroy it. The plan involved one of his most important generals, Reinhard Heydrich.

VILLAINS AND HEROES

Reinhard Heydrich was born in 1904 in Halle-an-der-Saale, Germany. His father was an accomplished musician and founder of the Halle Conservatory of Music; his mother, also a gifted musician, was the daughter of Professor Eugen Krantz, director of the Dresden Conservatory. All the Heydrich children had musical training and an appreciation of the arts. The family enjoyed prestige through its family name, Krantz, well-known in Dresden. Heydrich's parents were harsh disciplinarians, and Reinhard and his siblings were punished severely if high standards were not met. The result was Reinhard's obsession with perfection, his attention to minute details, and his drive to succeed in all he undertook.

When Heydrich was fourteen, World War I ended; but the young man was already planning a military career. In 1922, at age eighteen, he graduated from secondary school and joined the small, yet elite, German navy. His reputation for excellence was soon noticed, and he rose quickly within the ranks. Heydrich also earned a reputation as a womanizer. At twenty-two, he became involved with the daughter of a prominent German businessman. Accounts vary, but Heydrich cruelly rejected the young woman, who suffered a nervous breakdown. Several other of his indiscretions also became known. He was discharged from the navy at the end of 1930. Believing his treatment had been unjust, he became an embittered man.

By 1931, Heydrich had moved on to the National Socialist German Workers' Party. Later that year, he married a young woman with strong Nazi and anti-Semitic beliefs. At her urging, Heydrich joined the Nazi SS organization. Since that group was made up of young Aryan-featured men, it held great appeal for him: even in his youth he held the strong belief that blond, blue-eyed Germanic people were a supreme race. The main purpose of the black-coated Nazi SS was to act as bodyguards for high-ranking Nazi officials. This also appealed to him. When he was twenty-seven, through expert connivance and shrewd calculation, he advanced to new position, creating the Nazi intelligence organization known as the SS Security Service. He designed a file system, and using a conglomeration of informers, he began recording the names of every person opposed to Nazi ideology. Any small bit of information was carefully filed away, whether based on fact, rumor, or overheard conversation. High Nazi officials were not immune, and each indiscretion or flaw found a place in Heydrich's files. By the end of 1932, Heydrich had complete control of the SS Security Service.

In 1933, Hitler became Chancellor of Germany. What began as a boycott of Jewish shops and businesses soon became deportation, and then murder on a massive scale. With Heydrich's mode of operation in place, he made many enemies among constituents and colleagues within the Nazi party. Rumors spread that Heydrich himself was Jewish, through his paternal grandfather. Driven to prove this false, and maddened by the rumors, he soon showed a resentment and hatred for Jews magnified beyond reason. Although Hitler appointed Himmler as head of the new Gestapo, Heydrich was second in command; in truth, Heydrich ran the organization. The power of the Gestapo was without limits; all opponents were eliminated by means of blackmail, torture, and murder. So powerful was he that Heydrich was often thought to be Hitler's successor. Throughout the Nazi network, it was common knowledge that this man was calculating, manipulative, and totally lacking in compassion. All Europe feared him.

As Hitler's thirst for power escalated, so did Heydrich's. Czechoslovakia and Austria became victims of the Third Reich in 1938. Then a meeting took place in Munich with Hitler, British Prime Minister Chamberlain, and French Premier Daladier. Hitler demanded that the Sudetenland, a part of western Czechoslovakia, should belong to Germany since it was heavily populated by German-speaking people. He promised that his armies would not invade any more of Europe if this concession was made. Hoping to satisfy him and evade war, the statesmen signed the disastrous Munich Agreement in September 1938.

Early in 1939, a sabotage squad was sent into the Slovak part of Czechoslovakia. Within two months, as a result of this squad's promotion of panic and distrust, the Slovaks were led to secede from Czechoslovakia. Slovakia became autonomous, yet was viewed as a German puppet state by the rest of the world. During this process, however, an active underground resistance organization managed to emerge.

In the meantime, neither France nor England challenged Hitler for breaking his word as the German army arrived to "protect" Czechoslovakia from a crisis that the Nazis themselves had produced. World War II began in September 1939 when Hitler's armies invaded Poland. Then, the SD (State Intelligence Division), the Gestapo, and the Criminal Police and Foreign Intelligence Service all became one huge central organization. Reinhard Heydrich, as head of the Reich Main Security Office, gained control of all these infamous branches of the Nazi "security" services. Mass executions soon became commonplace, and spontaneous shootings, hangings, torture, and other brutalities annihilated innocent people. Entire villages and cities were enveloped in fear as Hitler's armies saturated the continent.

In July 1941, Reich Marshal Herman Goering sent an order to Heydrich to prepare a plan for the administration and financing necessary to carry out what was called "the final solution" of the so-called "Jewish question." By September 1941, Hitler named Heydrich his Deputy Reich Protector of Bohemia and Moravia. Heydrich was sent to Prague to orchestrate the elimination of the Czech resistance movement. Underground operations all but ceased, and the bravest of the resistance members lost their will to fight; their numbers were diminishing every day. The English-based Czechoslovak government-in-exile, led by President Benes along with officers of the Czechoslovak army, initiated a plan to rid the world of Reinhard Heydrich. They planned a highly dangerous and secret mission that was given the code name Operation Anthropoid, the success of which would mean the death of Heydrich.

Meanwhile, in January 1942, top Nazi officials met in Berlin at Heydrich's order for the Wannsee Conference. The purpose of this meeting was to plan the "final solution." Authored by Heydrich, the plan described how the Nazi forces would eliminate the entire Jewish population of Europe and part of Russia, meaning the death of over eleven million Jews. Adolf Eichmann recorded minutes of the meeting, but this record was edited by Heydrich before its release.

During these months of rising Nazi power, Czech and Slovak resistance members bravely planned their own secret operations. One large network of resistance fighters was formed by members of the forbidden Sokol under the name Jindra. They aided significantly to missions planned by the Czechoslovak military in London and provided safe houses for the paratroopers.

Jozef Gabcik, born in 1912, was the youngest of the four children of a Slovak mother. He was born in the small hamlet called Poluvsie, near Zilina, then under Austro-Hungarian rule, before the country of

Czechoslovakia had been created. Educated in a village school and apprenticed as a blacksmith/locksmith, Gabcik joined military service at age twenty, and served for five years in the Czechoslovak army. From 1937 to 1939, he worked in a chemical plant in Zilina where nerve gases were produced. When the Nazis became interested in the plant, and it was feared that the nerve gas stock might fall into their hands, Gabcik sabotaged a warehouse to destroy the supply. Facing arrest, he fled the country, joined the French Foreign Legion, and fought on the battlefront with the French. When Czech forces were established in Great Britain, he once again became part of the Czechoslovak army, operating out of London.

A dedicated soldier, Gabcik made quick advancement, soon being promoted to the *rotmajstra* infantry where he asked to be trained for special missions. Through an arduous process, he was chosen to take part in the top secret mission, Operation Anthropoid, and was sent to a special training station in Scotland. There he gained expertise in marksmanship and explosives and, by 1941, he completed paratrooper training. Gabcik was only twenty-eight when he was chosen to help assassinate Heydrich, and he knew that in all likelihood, he would not survive to see the results of the mission. Karel Svoboda, a Czech staff sergeant, became Gubcik's partner for the mission, and both underwent the same training. Svoboda, however, suffered a head injury during a trial jump and had to be replaced. Gabcik requested that his friend, Jan Kubis, become Svoboda's replacement.

Jan Kubis, born in Moravia in 1913, also realized that his chances of survival were slim. In his youth, Kubis was an apprentice electrician; at age twenty-two, he joined the Czechoslovak army. He attended a school for non-commissioned officers. Shortly before the declaration of the war, he joined a group of Czechoslovaks in Krakow and fought with Polish forces. He then transferred to Algiers, where he fought with the French Foreign Legion and earned the French *Croix de Guerre* service award. When the German army prevailed in the battle of France, Kubis fled to London where he became a member of the Czechoslovak army-in-exile, training as a paratrooper with his friend, Jozef Gabcik. Eager for a special mission, he became an accomplice in the plan to assassinate Reinhard Heydrich.

For many months of intense planning and drilling, coupled with endless surveillance work by members of the underground, the Operation Anthropoid team perfected the skills needed to carry out their urgent and deadly mission.

ASSASSINATION AND ITS AFTERMATH

Although Gabcik and Kubis were dropped into enemy territory in December 1941, all conditions for Operation Anthropoid were not satisfactory until the month of May in the following year. Gabcik and Kubis remained undercover for all that time, moving from place to place, with members of the resistance forces hiding them at great peril. Finally, faced with the possibility that Heydich was to leave the country, they took action mid-morning on May 27, 1942. As Heydrich drove to a meeting in Prague, his chauffeur-driven car rounded the bend of a curve where Gabcik and Kubis were waiting. The plan almost met with failure when Gabcik's gun did not fire. Realizing the gun failure, Kubis acted quickly, and threw a grenade at the car. Heydrich had been wounded, yet he and his chauffeur exchanged gun fire with the paratroopers. Kubis was wounded by flying shrapnel, but he and Gabcik were able to reach temporary safety, along with Josef Valcik and Adolf Opalka, who assisted them in the mission.

Heydrich was hospitalized and did not die of his wounds until June 4th. The man who had earned the names of "Butcher of Prague" and "Hangman of Europe" and "the Blond Beast" drew his last breath at Bulovka Hospital in Prague.

Seven resistance paratroopers dropped into enemy territory for various missions were aided by the underground resistance people and had made their way to Prague's Church of Saints Cyril and Methodius. These brave fighters were betrayed by two of their own, Karel Curda, and Viliam Gerik, who implicated all of those connected with the assassination plot and supplied the Nazis with names of members of Jindra. This ultimately led the enemy to their hiding place in mid-June 1942. Their betrayals resulted in the loss of many hundreds of lives. Both Curda and Gerik stood trial at the end of the war, were found guilty of treason, and were executed.

Jan Kubis was one of three paratroopers who were on lookout in the choir loft when Nazi police stormed the church. Already suffering wounds from the earlier grenade blast, Kubis and the others took part in a fierce gun battle. Kubis died of his wounds and loss of blood shortly after the German army took control of the church. He was twenty-nine years old. Adolf Opalka and Josef Bublik died of self-inflicted pistol shots rather than be taken alive by the enemy.

Jozef Gabcik also met his untimely death that same day, June 18, 1942. He and comrades, Jaroslav Svarc, Jan Hruby, and Josef Valcik were all said to have saved their last bullet for themselves, and died in the crypt under the church. Gabcik died in his thirtieth year, and none of the other heroes were any older.

Many versions of this heroic story have been shared, many of them from completely reliable sources, but each has a small twist. More important, however, is the end result: Operation Anthropoid was a success.

THE REPRISAL

Hitler and members of his regime reacted with cold fury when they learned of the attack on Heydrich. Even before Heydrich died of his wounds, immediately after the assassination attempt, the Nazis threw up a giant invisible net over Prague and the surrounding territories. Massive arrests were made, and wanton executions by hanging, shooting, and torture unfolded. Over ten thousand Czechs were questioned and 1,300 people were executed without any proof of a connection to the assassination attempt. (Some accounts count loss of Czech lives during this time up to as much as 5,000.)

The Nazis deduced that the assassins had been trained in London and that they must have been aided by local resistance members. The Gestapo soon learned that two citizens of a village called Lidice had fled the country in 1939 and were rumored to be serving in the Czechoslovak army-in-exile in Great Britain. Relatives of these two men (Stribrny and Horak) lived in Lidice, further implicating the village. Through the interrogation of a captured parachutist, the Nazis also learned that Stribrny had trained as a parachutist in London. In addition, a letter intercepted by a Czech turncoat was read and misunderstood, providing another obscure hint at Lidice's involvement in the assassination.

Without any proof of guilt, the Nazis decided that the citizens of Lidice aided the assassination plot. With only a smattering of evidence, the entire village was selected for extermination. In an effort to crush the resistance movement and create an example for others who resisted Hitler's regime, the Nazis planned and carried out the destruction of Lidice and the grisly deeds against its people.

On the night of June 9, 1942, Nazi SS troops surrounded Lidice. By the end of the day on June 10th, the Gestapo orders had been carried out. Lidice's adult male population, along with all boys over the age of fifteen, faced death by firing squad at the Horak farmstead. Shot at first in groups of five, and then in groups of ten, they were later buried in a mass grave.

Children were separated from their mothers and taken away. The women were sent to concentration camps where many died before the war's end. Lidice's nearly two dozen Aryan-featured children were sent to a children's center, where six of them died. The others either stayed in the center or were adopted into German families. After the war, it was discovered that eighty-two of the other Lidice children were gassed in Poland during July 1942.

The Nazis attempted to wipe Lidice off the map. After personal property was stolen, they burned, dynamited, and bulldozed the homes, shops, school, and church. The river that ran through Lidice was diverted; the cemetery desecrated and destroyed. Those who were not in the village at the time, as well as relatives of the Stribrny and Horak families, were tracked down and killed. Following this massacre and devastation, Hitler announced these horrendous deeds to the world via radio broadcast, citing details of the annihilation. He proclaimed: "Lidice Shall *Die* Forever!"

Now, not a stake was left on a stone,
Nor the frame of a window sill
Where a woman could lean in the dusk alone,
Her arms aware of the warmth of the stone—
In Lidice, in Lidice—

—Edna St. Vincent Millay[1]

A similar fate soon met the people of a small hamlet called Ležáky. On June 24, 1942, when a radio transmitter was uncovered in a mill there, all of Ležáky's inhabitants were tracked down and killed. The Nazis destroyed the village completely. Two young sisters, Jarmila and Marie Stulikova, escaped death since the Nazis thought they were suitable for Germanization. To further their attempts at ethnic cleansing, the Nazis also destroyed the small Romany (gypsy) camp of Lety, in the Pisek District, murdering all of its inhabitants.

A SHOCKED WORLD

The news of the destruction of Lidice and the fate of its people spread quickly around the world. The Nazis filmed the massacre and destruction and forced its viewing on thousands to spread fear throughout Europe. Lidice was meant to serve as a warning to anyone who dared resist the Third Reich.

Instead, Lidice became an inspiration to all those who would fight until the Nazi threat was extinguished. Shock and outrage reverberated throughout the world; good people everywhere responded with disbelief and horror. Although many villages, towns, and cities in war-torn Europe suffered, no atrocity was as overwhelming as that at Lidice. The name of Lidice became a symbol for all; a new and stronger determination to defeat the Third Reich was grounded in the name LIDICE!

Citizens of every country active in resisting the Nazis built up organizations to aid war efforts. When news of the Lidice tragedy became known, the floodgates of compassion opened. Soon, a new determination to defeat the enemy emerged.

KINDRED SPIRITS IN THE UNITED STATES

Pittsburgh, Pennsylvania

An impressive response began in Pittsburgh, Pennsylvania, which was heavily populated by both Czech and Slovak immigrants. Pittsburgh had been the place where Czech and Slovak statesmen came together in 1918, signing the Pittsburgh Agreement that led to the creation of the country called Czechoslovakia. Here a large number of patriots in the "Women of Foreign Origin" groups raised funds to purchase an ambulance plane. They named it the "Spirit of Lidice," in memory of the devastated village. More than $225,000 in war bonds were sold through their "Lidice booth," mostly by women with roots in Czechoslovakia. The "Spirit of Lidice" brought medical supplies and assistance to U.S. military personnel at the battlefront. It carried doctors and nurses to and from the scenes of battle, and transported wounded soldiers to hospitals in England and France.

The goal of this benevolent group was to continue the use of the "Spirit of Lidice" after the war ended. They hoped to bring aid and comfort to the countries damaged during the war in Europe, and to assist in the restoration and rebuilding of cities.

Phillips, Wisconsin

My own hometown of Phillips, Wisconsin, well-known for the number of its Czech and Slovak immigrants, became an important place in North America for the remembrance of what happened at Lidice. How did this come about? Many Czechs and Slovaks emigrated from Eastern Europe at the turn of the twentieth century, at the time that they were subjects under Austro-Hungarian rule. Since they had much in common, these immigrants gravitated toward each other in their newly-adopted land. Their languages were not exactly the same, but they understood each other. A large number of them settled in Price County, Wisconsin. Churches, schools, and fraternal organizations were created and shared by these new Americans. Strangers in a new land, they took comfort in the enjoyment of familiar and traditional activities with people who understood them.

"Women of Foreign Origin" group in Pittsburgh, with their "Spirit of Lidice" war bond effort

For my family and friends in the Phillips area, news of relatives and friends (and written contact with them) lessened as political strife increased in Europe. When World War I ended, the fall of the Austro-Hungarian Empire came with it. It meant Czechs and Slovaks could speak their own languages freely, worship as they pleased, and were no longer bound by strict military conscription laws. Members of the Slovak League of America, the Czech National Association, and the Union of Czech Catholics met in Pittsburgh, Pennsylvania, and in 1918, laid the groundwork for a new, independent country called Czechoslovakia.

At the same time, my town was typical in its devotion to the Sokol ideology. A gymnastics group (Sokol) met faithfully for many years. Goals set forth in 1862 at the inception of the Sokol ideology in Europe included sustaining healthy minds and bodies into old age. Patriotism played a large part in the Sokol tradition. These Sokol ideals and goals accompanied immigrants to America, and they also followed those who settled in Phillips.

In 1927, Phillips Sokol members were pleased to find a permanent home in a former school building. It was a meeting place and location for gymnastic practices, exhibitions, card parties, theatrical performances *(divadloes),* and dance parties *(zabavas).* This center became a home-away-from-home for many of the closely-knit members of the Czech and Slovak community. Our immigrant ancestors had known these familiar activities in former times, and many thought the Sokol ideal was among the better parts of the lives they brought with them to this new land.

Many who frequented Sokol Hall in Phillips did so as members of the Z.C.B.J., *Zapadni Cesko Bratrska Jednota,* the Western Czech Brotherhood Association. This was a fraternal organization established for Czechs only in 1897 when it split away from the Czech-Slovak Protective Society. Headquartered in Cedar Rapids, Iowa, it would later become known as the Western Fraternal Life Association. This fraternal benefit society provided burial funds, assistance for widows and children, and support from fellow members. Social and ethnic events became one way to preserve Czech heritage within this fellowship. In time, membership opened to others who supported the ideals and aims of the society.

In 1930, after the Phillips Sokol group occupied its building for little more than three years, the property was given by the Gymnastic Association (Sokol) of Phillips to the Czecho-Slovak Hall Association. Czech and Slovak Americans continued to be bound together in this small community, and the building became known as Sokol Hall.

These people established themselves in businesses, trades, and farms in the Phillips area. Though life was frequently a struggle for them, these immigrants treasured the religious and political freedom and the ownership of land in their new country. Those, and memories of mandatory Austro-Hungarian military conscription made all their new efforts worthwhile. The newly-settled people embraced their new land, anxious to call it their own. They filed Declarations of Intent, swore allegiance to the United States, became citizens, and struggled with the English language. Although anxious to assimilate, they welcomed cherished letters from those in the

*Temporary Lidice monument in Phillips, Wisconsin, U.S.A.
Left to right: Frank Hrda, Frank Koci, Sr., Ludmilla Urban,
Mrs. Frank Rehak, Joseph Skomaroske, Karel Novy, and Vaclav Hajny*

old country, written in the language they knew so well. Welcome also were ethnic newspapers that were passed from family to family.

In September 1939, Great Britain and France declared war on Germany. In December 1941, the United States joined the Allied Forces. Foreign-born parents in America saw their sons, and in some cases their daughters, off to war. Their concerns became two-fold: for their children and for those they had left behind in Europe.

In Phillips, when news of Lidice was heard on the radio, friends met on the streets, in stores, and at Sokol Hall. Theirs was a very personal pain. They were sickened to hear about the indescribably inhumane events. Many surnames of the victims were identical to their own: Dolezal, Dvorak, Fojtik, Horak, Podhora, Pospisil, Rames, Straka, Suchy, Urban, Vokoun, Zeman, Novotny, Novy. With a sense of anger, helplessness, and despair, once heads began to clear, they made a plan to memorialize Lidice in their own village. Knowing that the intended symbolic memorial would take time to build, they created a temporary monument that was viewed for the first time in July 1943.

This first Lidice Memorial Service in Phillips was attended by members of several Z.C.B.J. Lodges in Price County, and by many citizens from the area. A strong Sokol faction was present. Sokol members were aware that Sokol activities and doctrines could no longer be practiced without grave consequences in Nazi-occupied Czechoslovakia. This awareness made freedom and the call to patriotism even more precious to the Sokol membership in the rest of the world; it became one more element in the desire to defeat the Nazis.

This 1943 memorial service took place in Phillips outside on the Sokol Hall grounds, at the future site of what would later become the permanent Lidice Monument. The temporary monument was unveiled and both the American and Czechoslovak anthems were sung. Members of the lodge mourned the atrocity, and the somber ceremony ended with people leaving for their homes, rather than gathering in Sokol Hall.

The planners in Phillips wanted their permanent memorial to Lidice to be significant—to convey their heartfelt hope that those who died at Lidice had found peace and everlasting life. The tragedy needed to be marked in such a way that the world would never forget what happened. My community wanted its Phillips Lidice Monument to be substantial and uplifting in its message to the world.

The permanent Lidice Memorial in Phillips was completed in 1944. Both monuments had been designed by Vaclav Hajny, a Czech immigrant who was a professional commercial artist. His father had been a coal miner and once lived in Lidice. Another Czech, Karel Novy, was the mason who sculpted the work. Members of the Sokol organization and Z.C.B.J. assisted with manpower. Joe Skomaroske, local blacksmith, forged the letters "LIDICE" in bronze and iron, which were placed across the top of the memorial stones.

Some carefully-considered concepts helped create the symbolism that is included in the Phillips monument. A large silo-like pillar symbolizes the United Nations. Three rods fused into the pillar portray the Czech, Slovak, and Moravian people leaning on the U.N. for support. A large evergreen spray on the face of the monument portrays everlasting life for the brave people of Lidice. A molded stone circle symbolizes the rising sun—to indicate that the people of Lidice and Czechoslovakia will rise again.

On Sunday, August 27, 1944, at 2:00 in the afternoon, a large crowd attended the official unveiling of the Phillips monument and its dedication on the grounds of Sokol Hall; a fitting site for the people of Lidice to be remembered. A hushed and somber audience viewed the stonework for the first time, as a large curtain was drawn open to reveal the monument and those who took part in the pageantry. (See cover photo.) A uniformed Phillips High School Band performed, and Laddie Peroutka and his Internationals provided additional music. The speakers that day were Frank Hrda, president of the Lidice Memorial Association, Otto A. Jakoubek, Vincent Vrdsky, Secretary of the Wisconsin Czech American National Alliance, and John Panek, from the WCANA, Milwaukee, Wisconsin. Mr. Panek reminded the crowd that the Phillips memorial was the first erected by citizens of Czech and Slovak origins in the U.S.A.

Following World War II, Maria Kucaba and Anton Brendel, citizens of Price County and both immigrants, traveled to the land of their birth and visited the area that had once been Lidice. Each of them brought back soil from the old village. The soil was placed in a small vault with a list of names of those who made contributions for the monument, as well as the names of those workers who helped prepare its surface. The capsule was buried at the base of the monument during an annual memorial service.

The Original Lidice Memorial Vault

In 1967, twenty-five years after the destruction of Lidice, Jaroslav Ondres, a member of the Czechoslovak Embassy staff in Washington, D.C., was the guest speaker at the annual memorial service in Phillips.

Phillips' 25th Anniversary
Left to right: Speaker, Jaroslav Ondres, Czechoslovak Embassy, Washington, D.C.; Phillips Mayor, William Zeman and George Suchy

In 1974, by resolution of the Czecho-Slovak Hall Association membership, ownership of the Sokol Hall grounds and the monument was turned over to the City of Phillips. By mutual consent, Phillips became responsible for the maintenance of the monument and agreed to preserve and protect it. A stipulation was added that the land would be maintained and used for public purposes. Sokol Hall was by then in disrepair and was soon torn down. It was a sad day for those who had found such camaraderie at the Hall, but consolation was found in knowing that the Lidice Monument would have perpetual care and that a neighborhood park was being planned. In time, the area gained playground equipment, a ball diamond, and picnic tables. It was given the name Sokol Park.

A bit later, WFLA Lodge 236 furnished funds to have a bronze plaque made and fastened near the side of the monument. Its message briefly explains the Lidice tragedy.

Repair work became necessary after the monument sustained damage during a 1977 windstorm. It wasn't until 1983, that the repair work was completed, and members of the City of Phillips Common Council called for a rededication ceremony. That summer some young children, while at play near the monument, noticed the exposed vault. Weather elements had destroyed the cover of the receptacle in which it was buried and the vault was removed. In July 1984 a rededication ceremony and memorial service were held. Laddie Zellinger acted as chairman of the memorial service, and maintained that position for over ten years.

— 25

Joseph Ondracek was the guest speaker at the 1984 rededication ceremony. A resident of Milwaukee, Wisconsin, at the time, Mr. Ondracek was instrumental in reuniting the missing children of Lidice and Ležáky with their families after the war. He served on an international team formed expressly for that purpose by the Czechoslovak government.

1984 Rededication Ceremony, Joseph Ondracek, speaker

As a result of the meetings to plan the 1984 rededication service, second and third-generation Czech and Slovak Americans began meeting to form the Phillips Czechoslovakian Community Festival Committee. Since 1984, an annual festival takes place in Phillips each full third weekend in June. A Lidice memorial service is an important part of the weekend events every year.

In 1986, Joseph Ondracek places a wreath at the Lidice Monument.

1986 Memorial Service
Left to right: Joseph Ondracek, honored guest; Donald Johanek, Joseph Loula, Shelley Johanek, Charles Vich, and Lt. Col. Karl T.A. Moravek, Ret., guest speaker. Mr. Loula and Mr. Vich assisted with building the Lidice Monument in Phillips. The Johaneks presented the Lidice Memorial wreath.

A new vault with items of interest to the Czech and Slovak populations of Phillips was buried at the base of the monument in 1990.

Following the fall of Communism, Joseph Ondracek received an invitation to attend a memorial service honoring Ležáky in 1990. He also visited Lidice and was reunited with the children, now adults, which he brought home after the war. On his return to Phillips, the following year, he requested that a plaque honoring Ležáky be added to the Lidice Monument.

The Lidice Monument appears on both the Wisconsin and National Registers of Historic Places.

His own generous contribution, along with funds from the Phillips Czechoslovakian Community Festival Committee, made that possible.

In June 1992, Joseph Ondracek again returned to his homeland; this time, as a guest of the people of Lidice and their government. On June 10th, he took part in a memorial service that was also attended by Czech President Vaclav Havel. Fifty years had passed since the tragedy, and the service commemorated the brave people of Lidice.

In January 2006, through the efforts of Therese Trojak, Price County Historian, the Phillips Lidice Monument was listed on the Wisconsin State Register of Historic Places. In April of that same year, the monument was also added to the National Register of Historic Places by the U.S. Department of the Interior.

In 2009, the original vault containing soil from the old village was enclosed in an oak display case, designed and built by Ron Koerner. The exhibition is located for public viewing at the Phillips City Library.

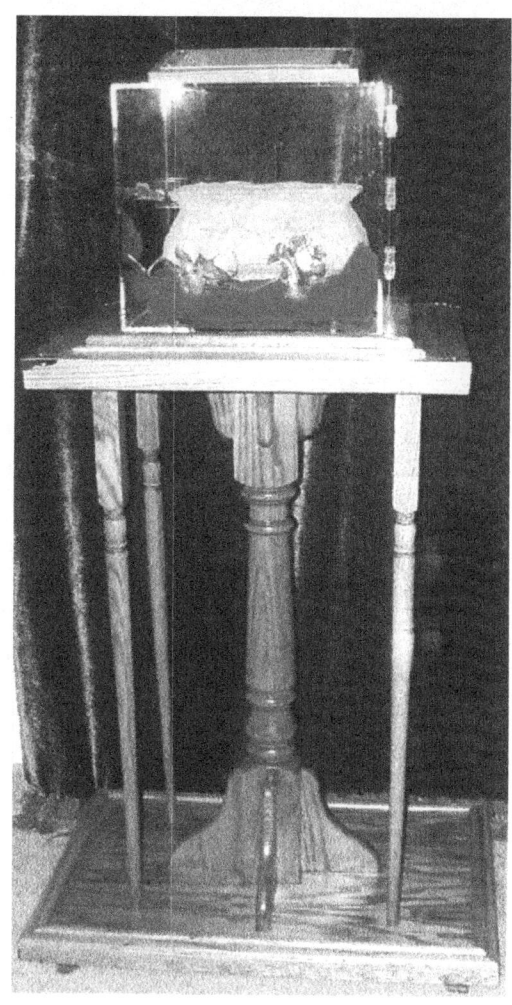

Soil urn sent from the village of Lidice

In 2010, Lidice's mayor, Tomas Skala, along with some of the citizens of Lidice, sent soil from the new village of Lidice to Phillips. This precious package went through the proper governmental channels in both countries, and the soil arrived in Phillips just days before the annual Lidice Memorial Service in June 2010. It was fitting that the great-granddaughters of the two Czech immigrants who brought soil from the devastated village presented the new soil to the citizens of Phillips. The Phillips mayor and the president of the Phillips Czechoslovakian Community Festival Committee accepted the soil from the rebuilt village in a brief ceremony during the annual memorial service.

City of CREST HILL
Illinois

1610 PLAINFIELD ROAD, CREST HILL, ILLINOIS 60403 PHONE

Raymond R. Soliman
Mayor

Christine Vershay-Hall
Clerk

Joseph Bobikiewicz
Treasurer

Ward 1
Scott Dyke
John Vershay

Ward 2
Claudia Gazal
Brenda Lelis

Ward 3
Tina Oberlin
Neal Sternisha

Ward 4
Charles Convery
Tom Inman

John D. Tomasoski
Administrator

June 3, 2010

Ms. Charlotte A. "Toni" Brendel
Coordinator, 2010 Lidice Memorial Service
336 North Lake Avenue
Phillips, Wisconsin 54555

To the citizens of the City of Phillips, Wisconsin:

It is my honor and privilege to send you greetings and good wishes from the City of Crest Hill, Illinois on the occasion of your 2010 Lidice Memorial Service. Our two cities share a mutual respect and admiration for the Village of Lidice and its people. We both continue to faithfully observe the anniversary and remember the events that occurred at Lidice on June 10, 1942.

Our celebration in the City of Crest Hill will be held on June 6, 2010 where we will continue to proclaim that "Lidice Lives": words stated on our original monument. We will never forget those who gave their lives at the hands of Nazi oppression. The atrocities committed at Lidice are a perfect example of good always triumphing over evil and right always prevailing over wrong.

I hope that I will someday be able to visit the City of Phillips, Wisconsin to see your monument honoring Lidice, and I also hope that you will be able to join us in the City of Crest Hill sometime soon.

Sincerely,

Raymond R. Soliman
Mayor
City of Crest Hill

June 10, 2010

Dear Ladies and Gentlemen, citizens of Phillips

We are very glad to hear that our countrymen in USA and citizens of Phillips still remember Lidice. It is an honour for us to send you soil from Lidice, to be a part of your program and this way can celebrate freedom of new Lidice.

At the same time is very important for us all the time remind terrors of World War II, especially for rising generation. We hope that this is the way how to never let repeat tragic history of Lidice and other similarily destroyed cities and villages across the world.

We hope it is successful thanks to survivors women and children from Lidice. They take part in commemorations at other cities and villages in Czech Republic, and other European countries and also make seminars with students about the Lidice history.

These days are still alive 13 children and 9 women. Most of them still live in Lidice. In the name of the survivors, their families and all people in Lidice,

Yours Sincerely,

Tomas Skala
Mayor of Lidice

Message from Lidice Mayor Tomas Skala (unedited)

THE CITY OF PHILLIPS
Founded in 1876

Daniel Koštoval
Charge d'Affaires, a.i.
Embassy of the Czech Republic
3900 Spring of Freedom Street NW
Washington D.C. 20008

Dear Mr. Koštoval,

On behalf of the City of Phillips, I would like to send greetings to you and the citizens of the Czech Republic.

Many Czechs and Slovaks originally settled the Phillips area many years ago. Only with their tenacity were they able to make it on this difficult land. It is these characteristics that helped the Czech people through the atrocities of World War II and specifically the tragic events at Lidice.

I have been honored in the last few years as mayor of Phillips to be involved with the Lidice Memorial Service. It is in these preparations that I truly learned about the meaning behind this memorial. The Lidice Memorial was finished and dedicated in 1944. It is now listed on the United States National Register of Historic Places and the State of Wisconsin Register.

Our monument also includes a bronze plaque commemorating the Village of Lezaky and was paid for, in part, by Joseph Ondracek. Mr. Ondracek was a speaker at our memorial service in 1984. I understand he was one of a few people who were made honorary citizens of Lidice.

I look forward to the possibility of welcoming someone from the Czech Republic Embassy at our Lidice Memorial Service in June 2011.

Sincerely,

Jeffrey V. Fahl

Jeffrey V. Fahl
Mayor

CITY OFFICES AT 174 SOUTH EYDER AVENUE - P.O. BOX 21
PHILLIPS, WISCONSIN 54555-0021 - PHONE 715-339-3125 FAX 715-339-3265

Memorial Service—2010

Left to right: President of Phillips Czechoslovakian Community Festival Committee, Dorothy Koerner; Mayor, Jeff Fahl, Valerie Erickson, great-granddaughter of Anton Brendel and Amanda Peterson, great-granddaughter of Marie Kucaba

The soil from the new village at Lidice now covers the soil from the former village. Lidice has risen again—just as the symbolism on the Phillips Lidice monument predicted over seven decades ago.

Commemorating the seventieth anniversary of the fall of Lidice, His Excellency, Petr Gandalovic, Czech Ambassador to the U.S.A., attended the 2012 Lidice Memorial Service in Phillips and was the guest speaker. Following the service, three flagpoles were dedicated at the Lidice Monument site—the American, Czech, and Slovak flags will now fly side by side at Sokol Park. Descendants of Czech and Slovak immigrants maintain a strong presence in Phillips and pay tribute with a memorial service each June.

Photo by Bill Ball

His Excellency, Petr Gandalovic, Czech Ambassador to the U.S.A.

Left to right: Donald Pafko, Honorary Slovak Consul, Minnesota; Czech Ambassador Petr Gandalovic, and Sally Teresinski, President of Wisconsin Czechs, raised the flags for the first time in Sokol Park.

Chicago, Illinois

In the early 1900s, Chicago boasted the third largest Czech population in the world. The well-populated Czech neighborhoods in the inner city were filled with laborers who made their livings in factories, meat packing plants, breweries, and in the lumber industry. The Chicago Czech Americans introduced the idea of building and loan associations that encouraged people to save until they could own their own homes. In time, because of a thrifty nature, Chicago's Czech Americans were able to move to the suburbs, where they had purchased property. Soon, Cicero, Berwyn, Joliet, Riverside, and other areas near Chicago had pockets of Czech population.

Whether in the city or the suburbs, these Czech Americans were drawn to activities they enjoyed in the old country. They stayed close to the people of their own faith and heritage. Most were Roman Catholics and found refuge within their church affiliations. Others were Protestants or Free Thinkers, and met people of their own beliefs. But these associations remained mostly within the confines of the Czech-American population. In addition to church related activities, card parties, dances, and other social functions, these Czech-Americans enjoyed a strong connection to the Sokol (Falcon) gymnastic organization, indulging a great desire for fitness, both mental and physical. Along with the patriotism ideal, the Sokol credo also promoted physical, spiritual, and moral strength, together with a firm and noble character.

C.S.A., the Czechoslovak Society of America, the oldest fraternal association in America, was of great assistance to the early immigrants. Not only did this organization conduct activities and provide benefits to those in need, they also sponsored programs to help immigrants in many additional ways. Many other Czech-American organizations were founded in larger cities as the need arose to address the challenges of assimilation.

By the mid 1920s, there were four main Czech language newspapers in America. Each paper had its own philosophy and kept readers abreast of what was happening in Europe. Neighborhood saloons were favorite meeting places where news of the day and politics were discussed.

The Chicago Czech population took pride that Anton J. Cermak, a fellow Czech, was elected mayor of Chicago in 1931. Born in 1873 in Bohemia, not far from Lidice, in what was then Austria-Hungary, Cermak came to the U.S. when he was only one year old. He worked his way up to the mayor's office and was credited with helping build Chicago's Democratic Party. He was the first foreign-born man to be elected mayor of the city. While visiting Florida in 1933 and traveling in a motorcade with President Franklin Roosevelt, Cermak took an assassin's bullet intended for the president. As he was taken to the hospital, he heroically uttered: "I am glad it was me instead of you, Mr. President." With Cermak's death, Czech Americans were devastated. They believed they had lost their voice in political matters. Twenty-second Street in Chicago was renamed Cermak Road in his honor. That honor was a source of pride for all Czechs.

Lidice (now Crest Hill), Illinois

Czech-American communities in Illinois were greatly impacted by the shocking news of what happened in Lidice. Within two days of the tragedy, Dominic Romano, a land owner working on the Stern Park subdivision near Joliet, renamed it "Lidice," in honor of the devastated village.

With the city of Chicago, less than an hour away, thousands of people attended a memorial service at the new Lidice. This first monument in the United States to remember Lidice was dedicated on July 12, 1942. Men and women dressed in native clothing *(kroje)* took part in a parade; a mix of American and Czechoslovakian flags were displayed. A bereaved Czechoslovak President Benes came from London to attend the dedication ceremony. Although members of the Czechoslovak government-in-exile had known that a price would be paid for the successful assassination of a Nazi general, they never imagined a reprisal of such monumental proportion.

Republican presidential hopeful Wendell Wilkie gave the main address; messages from political and military leaders from across the globe were shared with the crowd. The atmosphere was laden with sorrow, but the thrust of Wilkie's message was his resolve as he proclaimed, "Because the lanterns of Lidice have been blacked out, a flame has been lit which can never be extinguished." Reporters from most major U.S. newspapers covered the story of the dedication that day in July, just a month after the tragic events.

People came to remember Lidice and its inhabitants, and they sent a clear message to the enemy. As the flame on the monument ignited during the ceremony in Lidice, Illinois, it symbolized that the flame of freedom and hope burned brightly for all those who were victims of Nazi brutality. Lidice and its people were indeed remembered that day.

New Lidice citizens in Czech kroje march to a memorial service in 1942.

This first memorial service was held only one month after the tragedy, and the Illinois monument was erected in an empty cornfield. Eighteen years later, this area became part of the town called Crest Hill, but the neighborhood still remembers it as Lidice. Each June, chartered buses carry people from neighboring cities to attend a memorial service at the monument site. The buses still use the Lidice name on the nameplate displayed on their windshields.

Original Lidice Monument in Crest Hill, Illinois

Before June 1992, this Illinois site underwent extensive cleanup in preparation for the 50th anniversary of the tragedy. Chicago area groups contributed over $5,000 to help prepare the grounds for the event. Visitors from Berwyn and Cicero and other cities all came to remember those who perished, and also to celebrate the rebuilding of the village of Lidice in Czechoslovakia. These Illinois citizens are justifiably proud to have this historic monument in their neighborhood. In addition to remembering and celebrating, many in the area know that the monument also symbolizes what patriotic Americans believe in. This monument denounces oppression and brutality wherever it occurs.

In 1995, the monument was toppled by vandals and a new monument was erected and dedicated. The president of the Oak Brook Czechoslovak American Congress reported that most of the funding was provided by Chicago-area members of the Congress. Ownership of the new monument was turned over to the National Czech and Slovak Museum and Library in Cedar Rapids, Iowa. The people of Crest Hill and members of the Congress developed a small park that surrounds the monument, situated at the corner of Prairie Avenue and Hosmer Lanes in Crest Hill. Today, the Lockport Township Park District maintains the park. Several varieties of roses flourish in the park and represent a sampling of those plants that grow in the Rose Garden, in Lidice, Czech Republic. The goal is to grow eighty-two rose bushes to memorialize the eighty-two children who died in Poland after being separated from their parents at Lidice.

New Lidice Monument—1995

Crest Hill Lidice Memorial Service 2006—Consul General of Czech Republic, speaker, members of Czechoslovak American Congress*

United Moravian Societies' singing group*

*Nick Churnovic photos

The Lidice Memorial Garden and Monument*

The rose garden and fence were added in 2005*

Floral Tributes*

*Nick Churnovic photos

Nick Churnovic, Mayor of Crest Hill (2005–2009) addressed a crowd in 2007. Far left, Representatives from the Czechoslovak American Congress and Czech Embassy, Washington, D.C.*

Left to right: John G. Pritasil, President, Czechoslovak American Congress; Frantisek Gal, Czech Republic Deputy Consul General, Head of Mission; Vera A Wilt, 2nd Vice President, Czechoslovak American Congress; Raymond Soliman, Mayor, Crest Hill, Illinois**

***Ray Soliman photos*

Special tribute was made in 2012 on the seventieth anniversary of the Lidice tragedy as members of the Czechoslovak American Congress and others gather in Crest Hill to remember the people of Lidice.

The Crest Hill City Library houses a display recording the dedication of the two monuments. In the lower level of that building, a display case shows artifacts of Czech heritage. Those involved in the Lidice Memorial services kept a scrapbook containing written accounts of the annual memorial events

Tabor, South Dakota

The small town of Tabor, South Dakota, named a street to honor Lidice and its people. With a population of a bit over 400, the predominantly Czech community continues to celebrate its heritage in June each year with Tabor Czech Days. Czech businesses are still to be found along Lidice Street, along with St. Wenceslaus Church and Sokol Park. The name "Lidice" is constantly remembered in Tabor.

OTHER NATIONS REMEMBER LIDICE

Stoke-on-Trent, Great Britain

The idea for the slogan, "Lidice Shall Live," was conceived by Dr. Barnett Stross, a general practitioner from Stoke-on-Trent, England. When Dr. Stross learned of the tragedy and that Hitler had announced that "Lidice Shall *Die* Forever!" this was his immediate response. Many of the men murdered at Lidice were miners, and Dr. Stross inspired the miners of his community to raise money to assist in rebuilding the devastated village. In September 1942, a campaign to raise funds was started by the citizens of Stoke-on-Trent.

When rebuilding began in 1947, over £32,000 had been raised in England and sent to the Czechoslovak government. The plan was to build 150 houses in the village. Many other countries contributed as a result of Dr. Stross' leadership, and over £1,000,000 were raised to continue the rebuilding process. With the project well underway, Dr. Stross introduced another idea—to cultivate a large rose garden on the grounds where the village once stood. He called it the "Garden of Friendship and Peace." His request that citizens of the world contribute roses produced an unbelievable response.

In 1966, Dr. Stross also suggested that an art gallery be added to the Lidice memorial site. As a result of his encouragement, the Lidice Art Collection became a reality. Artists of the world were called upon to contribute their talents to the gallery. In 1968, a national children's art exhibition and competition was first held; it has since become an international exhibition, with as many as sixty countries represented and over 25,000 entries arriving from all parts of the globe. Theartbay Gallery, in Fenton, Stoke-on-Trent, hosts the United Kingdom's Children's Fine Arts Exhibition and Competition each year, and the winners have their works submitted to the international competition in Lidice. This competition is regarded as a living memorial to the children of Lidice and to all child victims of war.

All of these activities and events included in the Lidice Memorial Museum and Art Gallery are the result of efforts in great part by Dr. Stross, a Jewish general practitioner from Poland, who transplanted himself to Stoke-on-Trent, England. Dr. Stross was honored by citizens of Lidice in June 1957 when he was made an honorary citizen of Lidice. He was also awarded the Order of the White Lion by the Czechoslovak government, an award that honors outstanding support of the Czechoslovak people. Dr. Stross was also knighted in England in 1964, recognized for his outstanding humanitarian achievements. When Dr. Stross died in 1967, the citizens of Lidice mourned his death profoundly. This extraordinary man is still fondly remembered for the significant contributions he made on behalf of their village and country.

A strong and enduring bond continues to exist between the people of Lidice and citizens of Stoke-on-Trent today. A delegation of survivors led by Marie Supikova, attended the 70th anniversary commemoration and the unveiling of a memorial plaque to honor Dr. Stross in 2012.

Lidice, Brazil

In South America, a small town in Brazil in the municipality of Angras dos Reis, near Rio de Janeiro, was renamed Lidice. A monument was erected in the town square in memory of the Czechoslovak village and its people. See photo at right.

Nick Churnovic photos

Nick Churnovic photos

Others in the World Remember

Throughout the world, many cities, towns, and villages memorialized the original Lidice by renaming buildings, streets, avenues, and city squares—using the name "Lidice." This is the case in cities in Mexico and Panama. City quarters were renamed Lidice in Caracas, Venezuela; Lima, Peru; Regla, Cuba; and Gan Yaoneh, Israel.

Squares, streets, parks, schools, and organizations were renamed Lidice in Santiago, Chile; Montevideo, Uruguay; Callao, Peru; Molo, Peru; Havana, Cuba; Calbarien, Cuba; Valparaiso, Chile; Budapest, Hungary; Bogota, Columbia; London, England; Goll, England; and Bremen, Germany.

Newborns were named "Lidice" in memory of the village, and a hospital became Lidice General Hospital in Caracas, Venezuela.

Movies were produced in which the Lidice tragedy was the subject matter. In 1943, English director Humphrey Jennings created a documentary using Welsh actors called "The Silent Village." German-born film director Douglas Sirk directed an American film called "Hitler's Madman," based on Edna St. Vincent Millay's famous poem, "The Death of Lidice." Lewis Gilbert directed another version of the story in the United Kingdom in 1976: "Operation Daybreak." This movie has been recognized as one of the most historically accurate of these films. The film drama, "Lidice" was released in June, 2011, in Czech Republic. Director Petr Nikolaev along with producers Adam Dvorak and Robert Schaffer dealt sensitively with a screenplay written by Zdenek Mahler and the tragedy is revisited with more than one facet of the story portrayed by Czech screen stars. It was released in the United Kingdom under the title, "Fall of the Innocent."

Musicians were inspired to write music in remembrance of the village. Czech composer Bohuslav Martinu wrote "Memorial to Lidice" for full orchestra in 1943. Other notable composers wrote music and lyrics for soloists and ensembles in memory of Lidice.

In 2012, to commemorate the seventieth anniversary of the Lidice tragedy, an exhibition was organized at the Czech Embassy in Washington, D.C. Along with the exhibition, a screening of the movie "Lidice" was shown. The exhibition, entitled "Assassination of Reinhard Heydrich—Operation Anthropoid, 1941–1942," was designed by the Military History Institute of Prague and created by Michal Burian, Ales Knizek, Judita Matousova, and Eduard Stehlik. The display is comprised of nineteen large placards depicting the assassination of Heydrich, the story of the Lidice tragedy, and related events from the war.

Innumerable books have been written by survivors of the Lidice tragedy, by relatives and friends, apt historians, and in some cases, by people with only a vague connection to the village. In addition to those written by survivors, notable is a book authored by Major PhD Eduard Stehlik entitled, "Lidice: The Story of a Czech Village." Major Stehlik's work involved research at central and regional archives, libraries, and eyewitness reports.

John Fiala photo

A large cross marks the mass grave where Lidice men were buried.

LIDICE TODAY AND TOMORROW

The Lidice grounds were proclaimed a national cultural monument, first by the CSR government in 1962 and then by the existing Czech Republic government in 1995. The area where the village once stood and where the men and boys met their deaths is considered hallowed ground. An aura of reverence pervades the atmosphere as one looks across the landscape where there was once a thriving village. A large cross stands high above the mass grave to mark the final resting place of the grandfathers, fathers, brothers, cousins, sons, and the village priest of Lidice. The landscape is folded and sloped in a fusion of green with smatterings of trees, bushes, and closely-cropped foliage. It is impossible to take it all in without reflecting on the profound ramifications of the tragedy.

Lidice Memorial Grounds

A simple stone marks the Horak Farmstead.

The Lidice Museum is sparsely furnished with items that somehow miraculously survived the devastation. Most are mere shards or pieces of items left behind. Photographs, letters, a small girl's dress, and a shirt belonging to a lost paratrooper are some of the artifacts that remain. The most stunning of all discoveries is to realize that the front doors of the old St. Martin's Church remain intact. The church was built in 1352; it can only be imagined that a local blacksmith forged the substantial doors more recently than that. The Nazis used the doors to herd stolen livestock into their trucks, throwing the doors into the vehicle and, at some point, casting them out along the roadside where the doors were discovered and saved.

Within the museum walls, educational tours and multi-media displays provide school children with learning experiences that books cannot teach. Visitors from around the world tour the area and may witness the unfolding of the tragedy in a movie production called "And Those Innocent Were Guilty." All the messages presented demonstrate what horrendous deeds human beings are capable of and how innocent people can become the victims of madmen who seek power.

Rose Garden

Citizens of Lidice conduct tours. A few who lived through the ordeal themselves share their experiences. These people are dedicated to this endeavor and hope to impart to others that the atrocities inflicted on the people of Lidice must never happen again.

In 1961, changes in the Rose Garden created a place for the many rose specimens, then representing over thirty different countries. Patterns and colors were coordinated to enhance and beautify the museum grounds. Although weather and disease sometimes take their toll, the roses continue to bloom and flourish, providing at times a special setting for weddings and other ceremonies for those who feel a special connection to the old village.

One of the most moving of the monuments at Lidice is the sculpture honoring the children. This was the dream of sculptor Marie Uchytilova. Professor Uchytilova embarked on what became a lifelong journey when, in 1969, she began to cast in plaster the likenesses of the eighty-two Lidice children who were gassed in Poland. As her work progressed throughout twenty years, she came to consider it to be a monument to memorialize *all* child victims of war. Dying unexpectedly in 1989 before her work was finished, Professor Uchytilova did not live to see her dream completed. Her husband, sculptor Jiri Vaclav Hamfel, took up her work and completed the last seven of the eighty-two bronze statues. The completed sculpture was ready for public viewing on June 7, 2000. Mixed expressions of sadness and fear are captured on the faces of the young children and evoke a poignant reminder of their collective tragic end. They stand gazing in the direction of the mass grave of the village men.

A memorial designed especially for child victims of war

The two-story Lidice Gallery was renovated in 2002–2003, and stands in the middle of the new village. On its lower level, various art forms are on permanent display. Space is limited—although 335 artists from thirty-two countries contributed over four hundred works of art, only ninety-four of these can be shown at any one time.

Other cultural events, including concerts and theatrical performances, are offered frequently at the Lidice Gallery. A restaurant has been added to provide food and refreshments to visitors.

The annual International Children's Exhibition of Fine Art takes place each June, after winners are selected by an authorized panel of judges. Youth, ages four to sixteen, are encouraged to participate in the event that draws entries from over sixty countries. This is an art competition designed to be a living memorial to the children of Lidice. Winners of the competition are guests of the Gallery at a reception held in June, when medals and certificates are awarded. The Art Gallery provides an educational center for youth and a room for research projects. All learning tools are furnished to encourage and develop youthful artistic abilities.

A group photo in front of the Art Gallery
Left to right: Ivona Kasalicka, Tomas Skala, Vice Mayor of Lidice;
Toni Brendel, Marie Supikova*, Vaclav Zelenka*, and
Veronika Kellerova, Mayor of Lidice

*"Children" from Lidice

The Gloriet at Lidice

Marie Supikova and Toni Brendel stand at the Gloriet. Marie was a child survivor from Lidice.

EPILOGUE

Some have called Lidice a "sacrificial village." And, tragically, so it was. There was no way of knowing in advance about the evil chain reaction that would be unleashed by the death of a Nazi general, nor how dear the price would be.

In retrospect, one knows that the elimination of Heydrich ended his power to plan the eradication of European and Russian Jews. We know as well that, because of the heroics displayed by the Czech and Slovak patriots, the Czechoslovak government-in-exile became recognized as a viable and important entity, earning respect from those who doubted its existence.

Other consequences of Heydrich's assassination were far-reaching. Many more lives were ended than that of just one man—and more than the seven paratroopers who died at the church in Prague—and more than those who were involved in Lidice. Those are the members of the resistance movement who supported secret missions of the Czechoslovak army-in-exile and the Allied Forces. Those individuals are duly honored; without their existence and support, none of the missions undertaken would have met with success.

The names of clergy targeted for aiding the paratroopers are forged on a bronze plaque, along with the names of the seven men who died in the church. The plaque hangs above the small outside opening in the crypt where the stone is pock-marked by bullets. Bullets that could not penetrate the sanctuary, but that bear witness to the ferocious battle that took place in the name of freedom at that place on June 18, 1942.

Photo by Ivan Kauki

Photo by Michaela Bujnakova

Bullets pock-marked the front of the
Church of Saints Cyril and Methodius in Prague.

Photo by Ivan Kauki

*Saints Cyril and Methodius Church
where seven brave paratroopers met with death.*

In addition to Jozef Gabcik and Jan Kubis, the other five young men who died here are honored in what serves as a national memorial to the heroes who fought against the Heydrich reign of terror. The list of heroes follows:

> Josef Bublik—Bioscope
> Jozef Gabcik—Operation Anthropoid
> Jan Hruby—Bioscope
> Jan Kubis—Operation Anthropoid
> Adolf Opalka—Silver A (Operation Anthropoid)
> Jaroslav Svarc—Tin
> Josef Valcik—Outdistance (Operation Anthropoid)

Photo by Michaela Bujnakova

Lest they be forgotten, a small area has been set aside near the church to remember members of the resistance movement who died during the aftermath of the assassination. All 294 names are listed on bronze plaques.

The crypt of the church has been set aside as a small museum where the seven heroes were memorialized. Bronze busts of both Gabcik and Kubis are displayed along with photographs and artifacts to commemorate the bravery of the young men who died in the name of freedom on June 18, 1942.

An effort is now being made to turn the Kubis family home in Dolni Vilemovice, Czech Republic, into a museum to honor the heroes who ended the life of a Nazi general.

In Zilina, Slovakia, near the village where Jozef Gabcik was born, a bronze bust of his likeness honors his memory. The bust stands in front of a Slovak army barracks, across a field from the historical Church of St. Stephen the King.

All of these monuments do not bring back those who were lost, but these shrines honor our dead and preserve the sacred memory of them. They link the past with the present, and serve as a potent reminder that here were heroes bound together—suffering, dying, and fighting in the cause of freedom. That is why we remember them, and that is why Lidice is remembered around the world.

> *Good people, all from our grave we call*
> *To you, so happy and free;*
> *Whither ye live in a village small*
> *Or in a city with buildings tall,*
> *Or the sandy lonesome beach of the sea,*
> *Or the windy hills, or the flat prairie;*
> *Hear us speak; oh, hear what we say;*
> *We are the people of Lidice—*
>
> —Edna St. Vincent Millay[1]

Photo by Peter Kocemba

NOTES

1. Excerpts from *The Murder of Lidice* from LIFE Magazine (October 17, 1942). Copyright 1942, © 1969 by Edna St. Vincent Millay and Norma Millay Ellis. Reprinted with permission of The Permissions' Company, Inc., on behalf of Holly Peppe, Literary Executor, The Millay Society, www.millay.org.

ABOUT THE AUTHOR

A native of Phillips, Wisconsin, Toni Brendel has a great appreciation for her Czech-Slovak heritage. She is a founding member of the Phillips Czechoslovakian Community Festival, acting as chair or co-chair for twenty-three years. She continues to serve on the committee's board of directors. Toni initiated the Miss Czech-Slovak Wisconsin State Queen Pageant, serving as director for twelve years, and continues in an advisory capacity on the national Miss Czech-Slovak US board. Since retirement, she has written four books about heritage; she is currently working on a fifth title. She has made presentations to local groups and to university audiences in both the U.S.A. and in Slovakia. She is a frequent contributor to ethnic publications. Toni is also an active member of the Western Fraternal Life Association, Lodge 236, in Phillips.

For many years, music received the attention that writing does today. Toni studied voice under the tutelage of the late Lorna Warfield, former Director of the Milwaukee Light Opera Company and Children's Opera Workshop, Milwaukee, Wisconsin, and at the University of Wisconsin-Stevens Point. She performed as a vocal soloist in concerts, theatrical productions, and programs. She has directed community and church choirs, and provided music for worship services on organ or piano at several churches.

Toni is the mother of four grown children, grandmother of six, and once a great-grandmother.

Children at play in happier times in Lidice

Made in the USA
Las Vegas, NV
06 July 2025